Tai Chi

for ARTHRITIS & FALL PREVENTION* HANDBOOK

Dr Paul Lam

The US Centers for Disease Control and Prevention, other health departments and arthritis foundations around the world recommend this program.

* previously published as Tai Chi for Arthritis

TAI CHI PRODUCTIONS

First published January 2001 and reprinted June 2001
Revised and reprinted 2002, 2004, 2007, 2008, 2012, 2014, 2016
Over 100,000 copies sold.

ISBN: 978-0-9925128-8-0 (paper)
ISBN: 978-0-9925128-7-3 (ebook)

Published by Tai Chi Productions Australia and International:
6 Fisher Place, Narwee NSW 2209
service@taichiproductions.com

USA and Canada
serviceUSA@taichiproductions.com

www.taichiproductions.com
Cover design by Matthew Lam

DISCLAIMER

Readers should consult their health professionals before engaging in the activities described in this book. The author, publisher, distributors and anyone involved in the production and distribution of the book will not be held responsible in any way whatsoever for any injury that may arise as a result of following the instructions given in this book. Readers who engage in these activities do so at their own risk.

NOTE

This publication is intended for use in conjunction with the Tai Chi for Arthritis classes by certified instructors or the Tai Chi for Arthritis instructional DVDs—the 12 lessons. It is not recommended that it be used by itself to learn the program. The DVD is available through many arthritis foundations around the world or from Tai Chi Productions..

ABOUT THE AUTHOR

Dr. Paul Lam, an Australian family physician and tai chi teacher, is a world leader in the field of tai chi for health improvement. In 1974 he started learning tai chi to help manage his arthritis. Tai chi has improved his condition immensely as well as all other aspects of his health. He is passionate about bringing tai chi to as many people as possible. In 2010 Dr. Lam founded the Tai Chi for Health Institute to empower people to improve their health and wellness.

Dr. Lam has created a number of Tai Chi for Health programs that are easy to learn and can be enjoyed by all ages and abilities. Over thirty published studies have shown many health benefits of these programs. He has trained thousands of instructors all over the world. His programs have improved the quality of life of millions of people. The US Centers for Disease Control and Prevention (CDC) recommends the Tai Chi for Arthritis & Fall Prevention program for fall prevention. Many health departments, the National Council on Aging and arthritis foundations around the world support his programs.

Dr. Lam has authored several books and produced many best-selling instructional tai chi DVDs. He has participated in over twenty research studies on the health benefits of tai chi.

FROM DR PAUL LAM

I am so sensitive to motion that even watching waves on television makes me nauseated. Eventually I found out that to survive long flights, I needed to keep my eyes shut. It forced me to do some soul-searching. One day in 1996 as I flew home from the US, during fourteen hours of soul-searching, the idea of creating a special tai chi program for arthritis struck me like a thunderbolt. As a family physician and acupuncturist, I understood both Western and traditional Chinese medicine. I had extensive knowledge of the various styles of tai chi and the challenges of arthritis. Most tai chi teachers are not familiar with teaching people with chronic conditions safely and don't have up-to-date knowledge of how people learn best. I suddenly realized that it was my responsibility to design the best program for people with arthritis. I found a great team of tai chi and medical experts to join me.

I am grateful for the tai chi expertise of Julie King, Michael Ngai, Robyn Nicholls and Ian Etcell; the medical expertise of Professor John Edmonds, head of rheumatology at St. George Hospital; Dr. Ian Portek, prominent rheumatologist; and Guni Hinchy, a senior rheumatology physiotherapist. We worked closely to produce an easy, safe and effective program. I appreciate greatly the arthritis foundations and societies and health departments around the world that have come to support the program. We were really excited when the Centers for Disease Control and Prevention (CDC) wrote to me in 2013 about recommending this program for fall prevention.

I would like to thank the many people who have contributed, refined and improved the contents and presentation, especially Valerie Sayce, the first editor, and Linda Scott the publisher and Jennifer Price the editor of this enhanced and updated version. Numerous others—Tai Chi for Health Institute board members, master and senior trainers of the program, instructors, participants, students, friends and family—whose enthusiasm for the program is the reason for the program's immense success in reaching millions of people. Finally, I thank my family for their ongoing support, especially my son, Matthew, for his ingenious design skill.

Please note: This publication is intended for use in conjunction with the Tai Chi for Arthritis classes by certified instructors, with the Tai Chi for Arthritis online lessons or the instructional DVDs. They are available through many arthritis foundations around the world or from Tai Chi Productions (www.taichiproductions.com)—my company dedicated to empowering people to improve health and wellness through instructional material.

~ Dr. Paul Lam

CONTENTS

TAI CHI & ARTHRITIS

TOPICS:

- Why Tai Chi for Arthritis?
- About the Tai Chi for Arthritis Program and this Handbook
- Tai Chi
- Qigong
- Arthritis and Treatment
- How Tai Chi Helps Arthritis
- Fall Prevention
- The Scientific Evidence
- Guide to Tai Chi Practice

Dr. Lam working with US Arthritis Foundation with Dr. Patience White, chief medical director, and Jeannine Galloway, program director, 2008

WHY TAI CHI FOR ARTHRITIS?

There are many styles and forms of tai chi with significant differences among them. Traditional tai chi forms are complex; some contain movements with high risk of injury.

Tai Chi for Arthritis was designed by Dr. Lam with a team of medical and tai chi experts. It is easy to learn—most people can learn it in days, weeks or at most several months. It is also safe. All high-risk movements have been removed and replaced with ones that are more effective for health. In addition, certified instructors around the world are available to teach this program effectively and safely.

The program is proven effective by medical studies and supported by arthritis foundations worldwide. It can be practiced sitting as well as standing. Almost anyone, of any physical condition, can begin and continue to progress regardless of age.

According to traditional Chinese medicine, qi is essential for health and vitality. Tai Chi for Health programs are designed to enhance qi. Thus, practice of the forms not only improves the specific condition, but also benefits almost all aspects of health.

Tai Chi for Arthritis Instructors' Training Class, January 2017

ABOUT THE TAI CHI FOR ARTHRITIS PROGRAM AND THIS HANDBOOK

Millions of people with arthritis and without arthritis have discovered Dr. Lam's Tai Chi for Arthritis program. You can learn it by attending classes by certified instructors, using Dr. Lam's instructional DVDs or viewing online lessons (www.DrLamTaiChiLessons.com). Millions of people have gained significant pain relief and improved health and quality of life within a short time. Over thirty published medical studies have shown this program brings pain relief, improves balance and significantly reduces falls. That's why the Centers for Disease Control and Prevention, among many other health organizations, recommend this program for fall prevention and health. The Tai Chi for Arthritis Handbook is designed to assist you with your practice with a summary of the 6 Basic and 6 Advanced Movements with photographs. The Warm Up and Cool Down and Qigong Exercise are also included.

We added useful information about tai chi, qigong, arthritis, how to improve your practice and the program itself. Toward the back of the handbook you can learn more about the principles of tai chi, where to find out more about arthritis and its management and helpful resources such as books and DVDs. For more information please visit Dr. Lam's website at DrPaulLam.com.

Be aware that arthritis is different for everyone, so you should seek advice from your health professionals. If you are experiencing any difficulties with the movements in the program, discuss them with your instructor and medical professionals.

Dr Lam and friends at the Chen's Village, the birthplace of tai chi, 2015

TAI CHI

Originating in ancient China, tai chi is one of the most effective exercises for the health of mind and body. Although an art with great depth of knowledge and skill, it can be easy to learn and soon delivers its health benefits. For many, it continues as a lifelong journey.

Almost anyone can learn the Tai Chi for Arthritis program. It's inexpensive and can be practiced almost anywhere. The movements are slow and gentle, and the degree of exertion can be easily adjusted, making it suitable for people of all levels of ability.

There are many styles and forms of tai chi with significant differences. The major ones are Chen, Yang, Wu, Wu (different words in Chinese) and Sun. Each style has its own features, although all share the same essential principles.

The essential principles include mind and body integration, fluidity of the movements, control of breathing and mental concentration. The central focus is to enable the qi, or life force, to flow smoothly and powerfully throughout the body. Total harmony of the inner and outer self comes from the integration of mind and body, achieved through the ongoing practice of tai chi.

The health benefits of tai chi include:

- increased flexibility, muscle strength and fitness
- less stress and more relaxation
- improved immunity
- lower cholesterol and blood pressure
- better body posture
- integration of body, mind and spirit
- improved flow of qi (life energy)
- just about all aspects of health

The Tai Chi for Arthritis program is based on Sun style - one of the five major tai chi styles. Sun Lu-tang (1861–1932) created this style in the early twentieth century. It has unique qigong (the practice to cultivate internal energy) and a higher stance so that it is easier to learn. It has many powerful features especially for health and wellness. Sun style tai chi is beneficial and suitable for almost anyone and is complementary to other styles. It is exciting and fun going through many layers of depth with this set.

QIGONG

Qi is the life energy within you, flowing through specific channels called meridians. It is a combination of the innate qi you are born with, the qi absorbed through your digestive system from food and water and the qi acquired from the air you breathe. Qi circulates through the body, performing many functions to maintain good health. The storage house of qi is the dan tian, a small area situated three finger breadths below the belly button. Gong is a method of practice. Qigong is another ancient Chinese practice that enhances health and relaxation.

The concept of qi is fundamental to traditional Chinese medicine, where holistic health is related to qi. When your qi is strong and harmonious, you will have good health. There are many different forms of qigong but, in essence, it is the practice of cultivating qi and consists of special breathing exercises, often integrated with movement and meditation. Tai chi has incorporated qigong as an integral part of its practice.

When you practice qigong, you can focus on your inner self; this helps enhance relaxation and improve your tai chi. Dr. Lam's dan tian breathing method (explained near the end of this handbook) is an extra effective qigong combining ancient wisdom with modern medical knowledge.

ARTHRITIS AND TREATMENT

The word arthritis means, literally, inflammation of the joint, but in general refers to a range of conditions affecting joints, muscles, bone and connective tissue. Sometimes the overall term musculoskeletal condition is used. There are over one hundred different forms of arthritis and other musculoskeletal conditions. It is the most common chronic condition, affecting one in five adults. Although there is a considerable range of variation in different people's experience of arthritis, the most common feature is pain. People with arthritis usually have to modify their normal lifestyles because of pain, limited mobility, reduced joint function and the unpredictability of the condition. Many forms of arthritis are long-term chronic conditions. Good treatment is aimed at developing an effective management program.

Osteoarthritis is the most common type of arthritis, accounting for around 50% of arthritis. It is a degenerative condition of the cartilage that covers the ends of the bones and becomes more prevalent with age. Less common but more severe forms, such as rheumatoid arthritis, can develop at any age, most often in the younger age group, and are three times more common in females than males. It affects the whole body with painful inflammation and swelling of the joints.

An arthritis management program will vary from one person to another. Your medical practitioner, other health professionals and arthritis foundations can provide helpful information and support. The more you learn about your arthritis and the various forms of therapy available, the better you are able to work with your health professionals to develop an effective management plan.

You can find many forms of management and treatment such as exercise, medication, pain management techniques, complementary medicine, nutrition, aids for daily living, joint protection and surgery. With over one hundred different types of arthritis, they require different forms of treatment. Take time to understand the information and treatment offered to you. If you are not sure, feel free to seek a second opinion. There are arrays of complementary treatments that might or might not help. When using herbal or other "natural remedies," do bear in mind that what causes an effect to your body could cause undesirable side effects.

The Tai Chi for Arthritis program is designed by health and tai chi professionals to be safe, easy to learn and proven by medical studies to be effective. Be sure to check if your instructors are currently certified by the Tai Chi for Health Institute. All certified instructors will be listed online at TaiChiforHealthInstitute.org.

At the 19th Annual Tai Chi Workshop in Sydney, January 2017

HOW TAI CHI HELPS ARTHRITIS

Tai Chi in the Park organized by the Arthritis Foundation of Victoria, 2000

Exercise or being active is essential for good health, and it is even more important for people with arthritis. Pain and stiffness of the joints tend to discourage and even limit people from exercising. However, without exercise, joints become stiffer and muscles weaker, which will lead to further pain and stiffness. In other words, without exercise, arthritis gets worse in the long term. Exercise keeps bones, muscles and joints healthy, thus improving flexibility and muscular strength. Exercise improves the circulation of blood and body fluids through muscles, tendons and joints. Better circulation will aid the healing process.

Not all exercises are suitable for people with arthritis. An effective exercise program should have low risk of injury and fulfill three objectives: increase flexibility, strengthen muscles and improve cardiorespiratory fitness. Tai Chi for Arthritis can accomplish these and more, and that is why arthritis foundations and the Centers for Disease Control and Prevention recommend the program.

Fitness is important for overall health and proper functioning of the heart, lungs and muscles. Additional benefits include:

- Muscle strength: Important for supporting and protecting joints, and essential for normal physical function.
- Flexibility: Exercises to enhance flexibility enable people to move more easily. Flexibility also facilitates the circulation of body fluid and blood, which enhances healing. Many arthritic conditions such as fibromyalgia, scleroderma and spondylitis are characterized by joint stiffness and impaired physical function. Tai chi gently frees up stiff joints and muscles.

Tai Chi for Arthritis and Fall Prevention can improve all of these components. The program also focuses on weight transference, which improves balance and prevents falls.

Additionally, tai chi practice helps to relieve pain and reduce stress. This is accomplished in various ways. First, increasing muscular strength helps to protect the joints, thereby reducing pain. Second, improved flexibility allows for better blood and joint fluid circulation, which also leads to less pain. Third, tai chi is a mind/body exercise, which improves the serenity and relaxation of the mind and thus reduces pain and stress. As a result, those who practice tai chi often experience less depression and enhanced immunity, and improve many aspects of health.

FALL PREVENTION

Treatment of injuries due to falls is one of the most expensive health conditions. Evidence has shown tai chi is one of the two effective exercises to prevent falls. The Centers for Disease Control and Prevention (CDC) recommends the Tai Chi for Arthritis program, which is also called Tai Chi for Arthritis and Fall Prevention.

SYNOPSIS

There are many studies on measures to prevent falls. A recent review of 111 randomized trials involving over 55,000 subjects singled out tai chi and individually prescribed exercise programs by physiotherapists to be effective. True, tai chi movements appear to be gentle and graceful, but like the energy beneath a tranquil flowing river, tai chi has immense internal power. A great bonus at the same time is that tai chi also improves almost all aspects of health.

The world's largest fall prevention study in a community setting found that recurring falls were reduced by 67% in addition to many other health benefits. This program is also cost-effective. From a study conducted by Australian National University, the cost was estimated to be $56 USD per person per year.

Factors that make the Tai Chi for Arthritis program so effective include a high standard and consistent training of instructors throughout the world—one of the reasons for the CDC's endorsement.

Another extra benefit of tai chi is the reduction of the burden of chronic diseases. Investing in tai chi programs can provide cost savings in other areas. As the practice of tai chi improves many aspects of health, it can also be an ideal preventive medicine for all chronic conditions such as heart disease and diabetes.

For more information please see the full article on Tai Chi for Health Institute website (TCHI.ORG). For grant application see:

US. Administration for Community Living Falls Prevention Grantee Tai Chi for Arthritis Information and Guidance.

THE SCIENTIFIC EVIDENCE

There are more than thirty published medical studies showing the health benefits of this program. Below are three of these studies, but you can find all of them listed at TaiChiforHealthInstitute.org.

In September 2003, *The Journal of Rheumatology* published a study that compared older adults with arthritis who practiced tai chi to other older adults with arthritis who did not practice tai chi. After twelve weeks, those who practiced the Tai Chi for Arthritis program had 35% less pain, 29% less stiffness and 29% more ability to perform daily tasks (like climbing stairs), as well as improved balance when compared to the non-tai chi group.

Arthritis Care & Research published a study in April 2007 that compared older, sedentary people with chronic osteoarthritis (OA) of the knee or hip to those who practiced tai chi and those who did not. After twelve weeks of learning Tai Chi for Arthritis, the participants gained significant and sustained improvement in physical function as well as pain relief.

The largest study of Tai Chi for Arthritis, by Professor Leigh Callahan and colleagues from the University of North Carolina, shows significant health benefits for people with all types of arthritis. This landmark study was published by the *Journal of Aging and Physical Activity* in 2016.

In the study, 354 participants were randomly assigned to two groups. The tai chi group received eight weeks of lessons, while the other group was a control group waiting for tai chi classes. It was found that there was significant pain relief, less stiffness and better ability to manage daily living. The tai chi participants felt better about their overall wellness and experienced improved balance.

GUIDE FOR TAI CHI PRACTICE

The benefits of tai chi come with ongoing practice. Each practice session can be an enjoyable, relaxing and satisfying experience. Exercising with arthritis is not always easy and you need to find a balance between doing too much and giving up too easily. The following guidelines will help you decide when and where, how much, how to progress and how to avoid problems with your arthritis. Check with your health professionals before you start.

1. Set up a regular practice time, so your tai chi practice becomes a part of your daily routine.
2. Avoid practicing in a place that is too hot, too cold or is windy.
3. Practice in an area that is clear of obstacles, has a non-slippery surface and no loose mats.
4. Wear loose, comfortable clothing and flat, well-fitting shoes.
5. Do not practice when you are very hungry, immediately after a meal or when you are very upset.
6. Begin your session with the warm up exercises and end with the cool down exercises. These help you have a good start and prevent pain and stiffness.
7. Continue your session only for as long as you feel comfortable. Listen to your body and rest when you start feeling tired, are in pain or lose concentration.
8. Gradually build up the length and number of practice sessions, aiming for about ten to twenty minutes on most days. A simple indication of how long to practice initially is the length of time you can walk comfortably at a steady pace. If you can practice for just ten minutes in one session, you can do another ten minutes after you have rested.
9. Arrange to practice with someone else, especially when you are not feeling motivated. It would be sharing quality time with your friend(s).
10. Be gentle with yourself and stay within your comfort range for level of exertion and length of practice session. Some days you will be able to do more than others.
11. Don't continue doing any movement that is painful or causes you discomfort. If you experience chest pains, shortness of breath or dizziness or if additional pain in your joints persists, contact your doctor.
12. Take extra care to move with awareness and caution when you are having a flare up.
13. Talk to your instructor about any movements you are finding difficult or uncomfortable.
14. Do all movements slowly, continuously and smoothly. As you become more familiar with the movements, they will start to flow more easily and feel more graceful.
15. Stand up between movements if your knees become stiff or painful in the bent position. As your muscles become stronger you will be able to stay comfortably in the squatting position for longer.
16. Breathe slowly, naturally and easily. As you become more familiar with the movements, try to coordinate them with your breathing, as instructed. Return to your natural breathing if you find this feels uncomfortable.

17. Use the minimum effort necessary to do the movements. This will help you cultivate qi and to relax.

18. Imagine the air around you is slightly dense and you are gently pressing against this resistance as you move. This helps cultivate qi.

19. Practice the qigong exercise at any time to help you relax.

FOLLOWING THE INSTRUCTIONS

It is assumed you are learning all the movements of the Tai Chi for Arthritis program from a certified instructor in a class, or by studying Dr. Paul Lam's Tai Chi for Arthritis instructional DVD. This *Tai Chi for Arthritis and Fall Prevention Handbook* gives you an outline of the complete Tai Chi for Arthritis program to assist you in your practice. If you are unclear about a movement, speak with your instructor.

The easiest way to learn a complete movement is to first divide it into smaller sections, corresponding to the stages shown in the photographs. Practice the first section until you feel confident, then add the next one. Start again from the beginning, practicing section one plus section two. When you are ready, gradually add the next section. Always return to the constant starting point, like the lessons in Dr. Lam's instructional DVD.

The description of the Tai Chi for Arthritis program is divided into two sections: the 6 Basic Movements and the 6 Advanced Movements. At the beginning of each section, the names of each of the movements are listed. This may be enough to remind you of what comes next. If you need further guidance, the movements are shown more fully in the following pages.

Each movement is shown with photographs of Dr. Paul Lam in key positions with accompanying brief instructions. When you look at the photographs, imagine you are looking at Dr. Lam as though he is your instructor. The written instructions tell you whether you are using your right or left arm or leg for the movement.

Dr. Lam at a Tai Chi workshop in New Zealand, 2008

Tai Chi for Arthritis demonstration in Barcelona, Spain with Jef Morris and friends, 2006

THE 1-2-3 WARM UP EXERCISES

These special tai chi warm up and stretching exercises are designed to prepare you to practice tai chi by tuning up your muscles and helping you focus.

- Shake your feet and hands between every few movements.
- Always do the easy alternative first. Do the more difficult movements only when you're comfortable with them. Use a chair or wall to give yourself support whenever you need it.
- Move through the exercises slowly and gently, with attention to how your body is responding. Ease off if you feel any discomfort.
- Respect your comfort range and adapt each exercise to your individual situation. If you have any discomfort or doubt about a movement, consult your instructor, doctor or physiotherapist.
- Repeat each stretch three times.
- Stretch to about 70% of your full range for the first stretch, gradually increasing the amount of stretch each time.

STEP 1. ONE WARM UP EXERCISE

Warm Up Exercise:

Walk around slowly, clenching and unclenching your hands for 1–2 minutes.

STEP 2. TWO STRETCHES

We will do two stretches for each part of the body, starting from the top down.

Do each stretch three times, ensuring that you stretch both left and right sides. It doesn't matter which side first.

Use a chair or the wall for support if you have any difficulty balancing.

Neck 1

1. Head down—as you inhale, bring both hands up slowly.

2. Turn your palms and bring them toward your chest, push your chin gently backward.

3. Gently push your palms forward, then press them down slowly and exhale.

Neck 2

1. Lift up both hands, turn your left hand inward and push the right hand down near the hip. Look at your left palm.

2. Move your left hand to the left, turning your head slowly to the left, then come back to face the front. Change palms.

Shoulder 1

Roll your shoulders gently forward three times and then backward three times.

Shoulder 2

1. Inhale and move your arms slowly upward.

2. As you exhale, gently press your hands down.

Spine 1

1. Hold your hands in front of you as though you're carrying a large beach ball. Inhale.

2. Exhale, push one hand up and push the other hand down, visualize stretching your spine gently. Then change hands.

Spine 2

1. Hold your hands in front of you as though you're carrying a large beach ball.

2. With your knees slightly bent, turn your upper body to the left. Then change hands and turn to the right.

Hip 1

1. Stand with hands up in front of your chest.

2. Bend your knees slightly, placing your left heel out in front of you; push both hands back.

3. Step backward with your left foot resting on the toes, stretching your hands forward.

Hip 2

1. From preparatory position.

2. Bending your knees slightly, push your hands to the side as though you're pushing against a wall and stretch the opposite foot sideways. Then change to the other side.

Knee 1

1. Make loose fists. Bend your knees slightly.

2. Stretch out one foot slowly and gently. Punch out gently with the opposite fist. Bring your arm and leg back in and repeat on the other side. If you feel uncomfortable lifting your foot off the ground then you can stretch your knee while keeping your foot on the ground.

Knee 2

1. With your fists next to your hips, bend your knees slightly and step forward with one foot.

2. Shift your weight onto the front leg and as your body moves forward, punch out gently with the opposite fist. Bring your foot back and repeat on the other side.

Ankle 1

1. Gently tap floor with your heel.

2. Gently tap floor with your toes.

Ankle 2

Lift up one foot, gently turn your foot inward and outward three times, not putting any weight on the turning foot. Change feet.

6 BASIC MOVEMENTS

1. Commencing Movement
2. Open & Close
3. Single Whip
4. Waving Hands
5. Open & Close
6. Closing Movement

Starting Position

Stand with your body upright but relaxed: feet slightly apart, knees loose, eyes looking forward, chin tucked in, shoulders relaxed.

Cleanse your mind.

1. Commencement Movement

Stand tall without being tense.

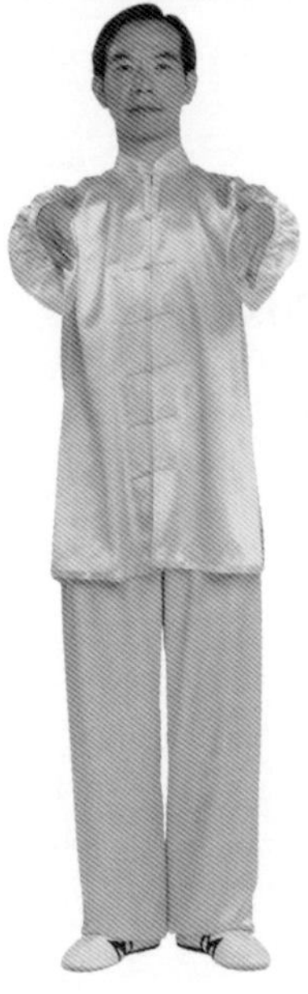

Breathing in, bring hands up slowly.

Breathing out, lower arms and bend knees slightly.

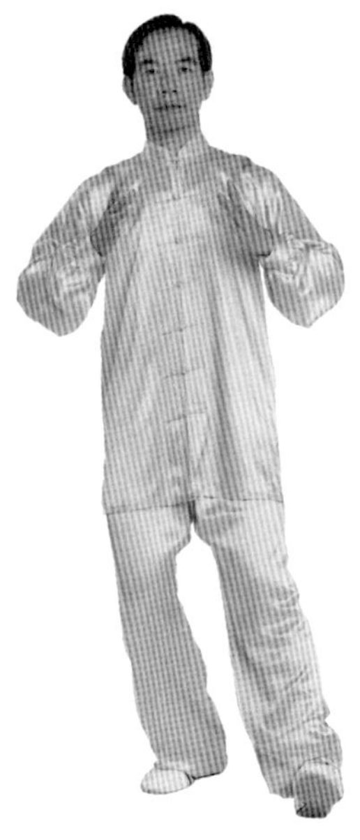

Lift arms, elbows bent. Step forward with left heel.

Push hands forward. Bring right foot in line with left.

2. Open and Close

Bring hands in to front of chest.

Breathing in, open hands.

Breathing out, push hands closer.

3. Single Whip

Step to right slightly forward, touching down with right heel.

Shifting weight onto right leg, push hands forward, turn palms.

Extend arms outwards, looking at left hand.

4. Waving Hands

Bring right hand toward left elbow, right foot closer to the left.

Stepping sideways with right foot, move right hand upward, left downward.

Move right hand down, left hand up.

Bringing left foot closer, turn upper body and arms to right.

Turn upper body and arms to the left, step out with right foot, then move right hand upwards, left downwards.

Bringing left foot closer, turn upper body and arms to right.

Move right hand down, left hand up.

Turn upper body and arms to the left, step out with right foot, then move right hand upwards, left downwards.

Bringing left foot closer, turn upper body and arms to right.

5. Open and Close

Bring hands in to front of chest.

Breathing out, push hands in toward each other.

Breathing in, open hands.

To continue: repeat to the opposite side, eg step to the left with left foot, do Single Whip Left, follow by Waving Hands Left three times, then Open and Close. After that, when you are ready, you can move on to the Advanced Six Movements.

6. Closing Movement

Stretch both hands forward.

Straightening knees and breathing out, slowly lower arms.

Keep practicing these movements until you are familiar and comfortable with them. You can incorporate the tai chi principles at the end of this book to improve your skill and health. When you are ready, move on to the Advanced Six Movements.

There is no rush in tai chi. You will get more benefit and enjoyment by developing your tai chi slowly and smoothly, rushing through more movements will give you less benefit and enjoyment - thus the paradox of tai chi.

6 ADVANCED MOVEMENTS

6. Brush Knee

7. Playing the Lute

8. Parry & Punch

9. Block & Close

10. Push the Mountain

11. Open & Close

12. Closing Movement

Follow-on Position

Skip the Closing Movements, flow on from Movement 5 and continue to the Advanced Six Movements.

6. Brush Knee

Watching right hand stretch out, bring left hand toward right elbow.

Stepping out towards the left, stretch right hand up slightly, push left hand down.

Shift weight onto left foot, turn body to the left, move left hand across knee and right hand close to the ear.

Push right hand forward and move right foot closer.

7. Playing the Lute

Step backwards with right foot, turning both hands inwards, stretch left hand forward slightly, right hand back..

With weight on right foot and bringing left foot back, move right hand back, left hand forward so that the right palm is facing the left elbow.

8. Parry & Punch

Step forward with left foot, turn right palm up, left palm down.

Transferring weight forward to left foot, push right hand forward and bring left hand back.

8. Parry & Punch (continued)

Stepping forward with right foot, turn palms over, right down, left up.

Transferring weight forward, push left hand forward and bring right hand back.

Stepping forward with left foot, bring left hand in front, right hand toward hip, then make two fists.

Bringing right foot half a step forward, punch forward with right fist over left wrist.

9. Block & Close

Stepping back with right foot, separate both hands moving forward.

10. Push the Mountain

Transferring weight to back foot, draw both hands backward.

Stepping forward onto left foot, push both palms forward; right foot follows with half a step forward.

11. Open & Close

Bring hands in to front of chest.

Breathing in, open hands.

Breathing out, push hands in toward each other.

To continue: do the Advanced Six Movements to the opposite side, then finish with Closing Movement.

12. Closing Movement

Stretch both hands forward.

Straightening knees and breathing out, slowly lower arms.

QIGONG EXERCISE

1. Stand with your body upright but relaxed: feet slightly apart, knees relaxed, eyes looking forward, chin tucked in, shoulders relaxed.

Cleanse your mind.

2. Bending knees, bring hands to front of chest.

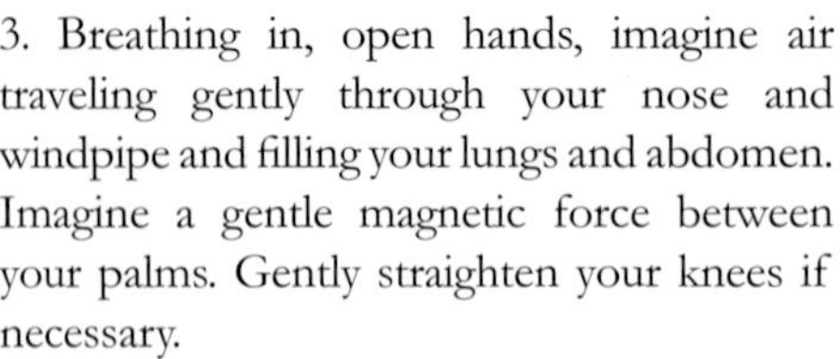

3. Breathing in, open hands, imagine air traveling gently through your nose and windpipe and filling your lungs and abdomen. Imagine a gentle magnetic force between your palms. Gently straighten your knees if necessary.

4. Breathing out, push hands toward each other, expel air from abdomen and lungs through windpipe and nose.

Imagine pushing against a gentle resistance.

Bend your knees slightly if you have straightened them during the previous movement.

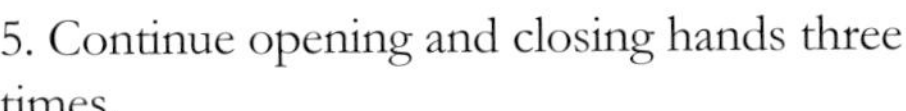

5. Continue opening and closing hands three times.

Complete the exercise by stretching hands forward.

After you became familiar with it, incorporate my dan tian breathing method (near the end of this handbook) for further development.

6. Return to original position, lowering arms and straightening knees.

Yin and yang are polar opposites of each other. There is a bit of yin inside yang and a bit of yang inside yin; both sides complement each other and together form a perfect whole. Yin and yang are found in all things in life and those which are perfectly balanced and in harmony will be at peace. Thus, a perfectly harmonious person will show this balance and completeness through tranquility and peacefulness of mind.

COOL DOWN EXERCISES

STEP 3. COOL DOWN

1. Punching thighs

Lift your thigh to a comfortable height and gently punch it

2. Tense and relax

Inhale, clench your hands, gently contract the muscles of your body, and stand on your toes if you can.

Exhale, letting everything go and relax.

3. Raise hands

Inhale and move your hands upward.
As you exhale, gently press your hands down.

Seated Tai Chi for Arthritis, Waving Hands pose, Florida, 2012

MORE ABOUT TAI CHI

TAI CHI PRINCIPLES

Tai chi was created based on traditional Chinese medicine, martial arts and the law of nature known as the "Tao." It incorporated knowledge going back thousands of years in Chinese history. In recent years, over five hundred medical studies have shown tai chi improves muscular strength, flexibility and fitness as well as improves relaxation, balance and immunity and offers other health benefits. However, studies don't show anywhere near the full extent of the benefits tai chi can bring, such as empowering you to develop serenity, inner strength and power, which leads to more happiness and fulfilment.

The secret of tai chi's near-magical effect for health and wellness is the principles that all tai chi forms follow. They might seem simple but are profound. Regular practice will enable you to discover the many layers of depth to develop your tai chi. These principles are divided into three main categories.

Lewis, age 92, and Mohammed, age 25, at the Tai Chi for Energy workshop in Colorado USA, 2014

1. Movement Control

- Tai chi movements are slow so that you can be mindful of them and integrate mind and body; they are smooth to facilitate serenity and they flow continuously like water in a river. The continual flow gathers inner energy like hydraulic power, growing as it flows.

- Move as though you're moving against a gentle resistance with every movement generating inner power. Another good way is to imagine the air around you is becoming denser or as though you are moving in water.

2. Body Structure

- Maintain an upright posture. Studies have shown that good posture strengthens the deep stabilizer muscles that support the spine. It also provides more space for internal organs. What's more, when you are upright you feel stronger and more positive. Qi flows better in a well-aligned body. A poorly aligned body puts extra strain on the spine and compromises your balance.
- Be mindful of weight transference and learn to do that progressively. Balance is an essential part of tai chi. Like nature, we are happier and healthier when in harmony.

3. Internal Components

- Loosen or 鬆 - song the joints. You should relax when you do tai chi, but by relax we don't mean let your muscles get floppy. Instead, consciously and gently stretch your joints from within. When your joints are song, qi moves smoothly and powerfully through. Tensed joints hinder the flow of qi and lead to stress. Song strengthens the internal ligaments and muscles, enhancing the function of joints.
- Develop a state of mental quietness or 靜 - jing. You are more mindful of the present and the self when you are jing, allowing your mind to be quiet from within.

EXTENDING THE PRINCIPLES AND FALL PREVENTION

After you become familiar with the Tai Chi for Arthritis and Fall Prevention program and work on incorporating these principles over time, you will reduce your risk of falls and improve your health and quality of life.

For some, different perspectives can enhance the understanding of the tai chi principles. Consider using mindfulness as another way to work on the principles. The more you understand tai chi principles, the more you will progress in your tai chi and gain more health benefits.

Be mindful of the following:

1. Breathing
2. Weight transference
3. Situation

1. Breathing Awareness

Tai chi breathing helps improve relaxation and balance. Incorporating the dan tian breathing method (described below) is a good way to be more serene yet more aware of the surroundings and thus prevent falling. Studies have shown fear of falling causes more falls. The breathing method will make you feel better about yourself, thus less fearful of falls and will improve relaxation.

Emotional state directly impacts your breathing pattern. If you breathe slowly and deeply for a few moments, you start to relax, tension leaves your body, you begin to feel at ease. When you become very distressed, dan tian breathing can help you to calm down.

Stress tends to increase our breathing rate. Increased breathing leads to taking in too much oxygen and releasing too much carbon dioxide. Since carbon dioxide is acidic, the pH levels of the blood decrease, disturbing our body chemistry. This can cause the blood vessels to tighten, which increases blood pressure. Prolonged high blood pressure has a significant effect on our health.

However, mindful breathing leads to a relaxation response within our body and mind. We literally can "breathe easy" as our blood chemistry and blood pressure return to normal levels.

THE DAN TIAN BREATHING METHOD

Dan tian is the area three finger breadths below the belly button and beneath the skin. This is the center of qi and the center of the body. This method is devised from the traditional tai chi abdominal breathing method, modernized with research findings of the deep stabilizer muscle and its relationship to breathing. It makes the tai chi breathing method easier and even more powerful at cultivating qi (internal energy) and increasing relaxation.

This breathing method enhances qi and promotes relaxation. Visualize as you breathe that the air travels through your nose, down your trachea (airway to the lungs), filling the lungs and then the dan tian area. Your abdomen is filling up with air, making it bulge gently outward. As you breathe out, the dan tian gently contracts. Physically, air doesn't enter the abdomen. This is a method using guided imagery to help utilize your diaphragm to open up more air space in your lungs, at the same time activate the parasympathetic system, which enhances healing and promotes relaxation. It would be even more effective if you could keep the chest and upper part of your abdomen as still as possible and only move the dan tian gently while breathing slowly. Relax your lower abdominal muscles as you breathe in, and gently contract them, along with the pelvic floor muscles, as you breathe out. Practice this as often as you can. You can use this breathing method almost anywhere. It is very important to do this breathing with an upright posture.

2. Weight Transference

Being mindful of your weight transference improves balance and posture. Correct weight transference depends on good dynamic and static postures. An upright and supple posture enhances mental alertness and strengthens the inner structures like the deep stabilizer muscles.

Be mindful of weight transference starting from posture awareness. As you move forward, put your weight on one leg while maintaining good posture. Touch down gently with the heel, then place the entire foot on the ground and then mindfully transfer your weight forward.

Try to stand upright but relaxed, look straight ahead, tuck in chin, and make sure shoulders, elbows and knees are song. Imagine the body as a string that is being stretched gently from both ends. Maintain posture awareness with stepping forward, backward and then sideways being mindful of weight transference.

3. Situation Awareness

Being mindful of where and what situation you are in at the moment makes you mentally more alert. Be aware of what situation you are in and focus on what you are doing. Walk with focus and be aware of where your body is and how weight is shifted. Be mindful of moving slowly and smoothly.

Apply being mindful of these three points at any time when sitting, working and especially when doing tai chi. If you teach this program, encourage your students to do so.

Practice better balance to reduce risk of falls.

Practice the 6 Basic Movements integrating these three points with the forms. Forms 1 and 2 (commencing movement and open and close) are best at incorporating breathing, 3 (single whip) for weight transference and 4 (waving hands) for situation awareness.

CONCLUSION

Practice and teach participants to incorporate mindfulness into tai chi practice and to apply it whenever possible. For instance, when waiting for the kettle to boil, try flexing the ankles or bend knees slightly and think of upright posture. Practice tai chi walking back and forth, mindful of weight transference, across the kitchen while cooking. When working at the desk, visualize wave hands like clouds and turn mindfully to reach objects from the left or right. Train your participants to think of the situation (where they are and what they are doing). For example, be aware of not overreaching, which may cause a fall.

When turning or stepping back and forth to appliances in smaller spaces such as the laundry, be aware of the transfer of weight from one foot to the other to avoid twisting a knee or ankle. When vacuuming or cleaning windows, move the body from the waist, not just the arms. Many tai chi students report that housework becomes easier this way. When watching TV, use the commercial breaks to perform the warm up or 6 Basic forms.

MORE ABOUT ARTHRITIS

Your local arthritis foundation can provide more information about arthritis and its management (much of the information is provided free of charge) and put you in contact with their many services (membership, seminars, courses, classes and support groups).

You can find arthritis foundations in different countries and localities around the world. Google your local or national arthritis foundation or society for their assistance. You can contact the Tai Chi for Health Institute for further assistance.

TAI CHI RESOURCES

Dr. Lam's Online Lessons
DrLamTaiChiLessons.com

An exciting new development is online lessons you can do from home, as though you are in Dr. Lam's class. You can access the lessons any time with a computer or mobile devices. You can join Dr. Lam's global Tai Chi Community to meet and learn from other tai chi enthusiasts from his workshop tour around the world. There are also regular updates, latest ideas, question and answer sessions, advice from tai chi experts and a forum to share with all master and senior trainers. There are so many things we can share at the online Tai Chi Community!

Online lessons would be ideal to supplement face-to-face class with certified instructors from Dr. Lam's Tai Chi for Health Institute. DVDs and books have many other advantages. You can use both to enhance. Using more resources will enhance your learning significantly. After all, health and enjoyment are priceless.

TAI CHI DVDS & OTHER PRODUCTS

We pride ourselves on producing high-quality, easy-to-learn DVDs. In collaboration with medical experts, arthritis foundations and diabetes foundations, Dr. Paul Lam has created a range of Tai Chi for Health DVDs dedicated to improving health and quality of life. He also produces DVDs for beginning, intermediate and advanced levels for those wanting to learn and better their skill. Each DVD is unique, containing step-by-step instructions with close-ups, repetitions, diagrams and different angles to facilitate learning. Many of the DVDs are worldwide best sellers.

Health Series

• Tai Chi for Arthritis
12 Lessons with Dr, Lam - 4 Hours
2 Disc, Handbook and wall chart also available.
The Centers for Disease Control and Prevention (CDC.gov), many health departments and organizations and arthritis foundations recommend this program for fall prevention and arthritis therapy. It is safe and proven to be effective. We invite you to take the first step on your journey to better health. Become a student in Dr. Lam's class in the comfort of your home as he guides you through each tai chi movement step-by-step. Anyone can learn this and enjoy the health benefits and tai chi practice.

• Tai Chi for Arthritis Part 2
6 Lessons with Dr Lam - 2 Hours
This more challenging sequel is designed for people who have learned the 12 movements from the Tai Chi for Arthritis program.

• Seated Tai Chi for Arthritis - *85 mins*
This easy, safe and effective program is suitable for people who are unable to walk or prefer practicing sitting down.

• Tai Chi for Beginners
8 Lessons with Dr Lam - 5 Hours
This shows the six easy steps to learn Yang style tai chi. Dr. Lam teaches the forms from different angles with close-ups, repetitions and diagrams to make learning easier and more enjoyable.

• Tai Chi for Osteoporosis - *90 mins*
This is designed to build strength and improve balance. It is an effective and safe program based on medical evidence on osteoporosis and fall prevention.

• Tai Chi for Diabetes - *90 mins*
Handbook and wall chart also available.
Designed to help prevent and improve the control of diabetes by gently increasing physical activity, cellular uptake of glucose and relaxation. Supported by Diabetes Australia.

• Tai Chi for Rehabilitation - *5 Hours*
Dr Lam has combined his medical and tai chi expertise to create an ideal program to aid recovery from ill health. Physical and occupational therapists may find it a useful tool for their patients/clients. Almost anyone can learn this program to help recovery from conditions including stroke, heart disease, injury, surgical procedures or tiredness and stress. Tai Chi for Rehabilitation will improve health and wellness after recovery. Also a great introduction to Tai Chi for Energy and Tai Chi for Diabetes.

• Tai Chi for Energy
8 Lessons with Dr Paul Lam - 5 Hours
Dr. Lam has carefully combined movements from Chen and Sun styles to produce a powerful synergy in Tai Chi for Energy. This program will help you acquire better health and wellness, internal energy and the ability to manage stress.

Intermediate Series

Designed to improve your skill and knowledge, this series is recommended for people with approximately one year's experience in tai chi.

• Tai Chi for Energy 2 - *Twice the Energy: 8 Lessons with Dr. Paul Lam*
This more challenging sequel is designed for people who have learned Tai Chi for Energy.

• **24 Forms** - *4 Hours*
Based on Yang style, it is suitable for people of almost any physical fitness level or age. The book T*ai Chi for Beginners and the 24 Forms* complements this DVD and makes learning much easier.

• **32 Sword Forms** - *95 mins*
This is a beautiful extension of the essential principles of Tai Chi, based on Yang style.

• **Sun Style 73 Forms** - *4 Hours*
Sun style is characterized by its powerful qigong elements, agile steps and flowing movements, ideal for developing inner strength and enhanced healing.

For our ADVANCED series and more titles, please visit our website at www.taichiproductions.com or contact us at 6 Fisher Place, Narwee 2209, NSW Australia.

Other Resources

• **Tai Chi Music CD**
Four beautiful and relaxing pieces of music composed to enhance Tai Chi practice and performance.

• **Tai Chi Music 2 CD**
Music composed exclusively for Tai Chi for Arthritis; Tai Chi 4 Kidz; Tai Chi for Beginners; and for the Chen, Yang and Sun Styles.

• **Teaching Tai Chi Effectively**
In this book, Dr. Lam presents the simple and proven methods to help learners enjoy tai chi, making it accessible to everyone. It is a must for tai chi or other exercise teachers to attract and keep more participants. It includes a guide to working with people of different ages and conditions from arthritis to Parkinson's, pregnant women to older adults.

• **Born Strong**
Dr. Lam's memoir. Share his journey from starvation and persecution to leading the worldwide Tai Chi for Health movement.

• **Tai Chi for Beginners and the 24 Forms**
This book contains step-by-step instructions and photographs of Six Easy Steps for the beginners and 24 forms. It also shows how you can progress to higher levels of tai chi.

• **Tai Chi for Diabetes: Living Well with Diabetes**
This book provides practical information on diabetes as well as the Tai Chi for Diabetes program with step-by-step instructions and photographs of the movements.

TAI CHI WORKSHOPS

Dr. Lam and his authorized master trainers conduct workshops around the world that are designed to be positive, enjoyable and interactive.

ANNUAL TAI CHI WORKSHOPS

The Annual Tai Chi Workshop is held in Sydney in January and in the USA every June since 1999, presented by Dr. Lam.

Dr. Lam personally teaches his Master Classes, focusing on exploring the depth of 73 Sun style, 24 Forms Yang style, 36 Chen style and other sets of forms.

- **Tai Chi for Arthritis and other Tai Chi for Health Instructor Training Workshop**
  At this two-day workshop you will learn how to teach this program safely and at the same time improve your level of Tai Chi. Many arthritis foundations and other health organizations support these programs and workshops.

- **The Depth of Tai Chi for Arthritis with Dr Lam**
  Dr Lam will show you how to utilize tai chi principles, understanding of internal energy (qi), internal force (jing) and the mysterious spiral force to enhance and develop your tai chi significantly.

Dr. Lam with master trainer Fiona Black (front row, left) and other Tai Chi for Arthritis instructors at workshop, Sydney, 2016.

For Questions:

AUSTRALIA and International
Tai Chi Productions
6 Fisher Place, Narwee NSW 2209 Australia
service@taichiproductions.com
+61 2 9533 6511

USA and Canada
serviceusa@taichiproductions.com
+1 906 217 2000

www.taichiproductions.com

Notes

Notes